A Journey
Along the Way

A Journey Along the Way
Inner Thoughts

By
Donna Banks-Diggs

E-BookTime, LLC
Montgomery, Alabama

A Journey Along the Way
Inner Thoughts

Copyright © 2007 by Donna Banks-Diggs

ISBN: 978-1-59824-556-1

First Edition
Published August 2007
E-BookTime, LLC
6598 Pumpkin Road
Montgomery, AL 36108
www.e-booktime.com

This book is dedicated to my sons,
Byron Kenneth Diggs II, Preston Stuart Diggs,
granddaughter Zariah Presleigh Diggs
and to all of my sisters, nieces and nephews.

A special love to the Kimble and Beckwith family.

To my Pastor, Marvin Connelly, Jr. Your love and
inspiration will never be forgotten.

Much Love

Contents

Contents

Abused

I saw them, the tears, falling from your eyes
The silent pain in your heart, I did recognize

I knew the face that abuse unforgettably show
A face of shame, guilt, a face hung low

Tears flowing like an endless stream of despair
Wondering where was the love, where was the promised care

You say to yourself, I can handle the burden, you put on life's fake
disguise
But others who have been there can see between the lies

You told me, you had bruised your arm upon the chair
But then you said you slipped on the stair

Then you said, the left side of your face had turn red
But it was actually his right handprint upside your head

At first you said, I feel a little sick, but not anymore
You never said he slapped you to the floor

Oh how your eyes are darken by worry and fears
Cause you laid upon your pillow and filled it with tear

Alone

Alone is a different place to be,
Nobody else, just myself, only me.
A simple place few people desire,
A place of refuge, for those traveled before can admire.

Not a secret passage, by way you go,
Nor a hidden door, by way to open.

A place to think, a place to feel
A place to rest, a place to heal

Find you there, joy, Find you there, peace
Find you there, strength, Find you there, love
Alone, with one's self.

A Different Feel

How would you feel, if those people who you had hurt along the way,
Was standing with God, at the pearly gates on judgment day.
Without a doubt, you know you would make it in,
You saw their face, you thought about the unforgiven sin.
Would you think they had forgotten, the day you hurt their heart,
Now their chance for revenge, to help God say from me you will depart.
Remember the day you hurt them your heart felt glad,
Now a different feel, on this day your heart forever sad.
It's because you know you're chances will be no more,
This is final, the last door.
No returns, never again to be,
In the fire, your soul tormented eternally.
Remember to repent for the things you do and say,
That you may find peace on judgment day.

A Dog Gun Thought

When you willingly place a gun in your hand
A thought to remember, a thing to understand
You aim to do damage and you aim to cause pain
After the trigger is pulled, there's no time for shame
A bullet has no mind, it knows no name
You're given a brain, intelligence to use
Not to destroy a life or a life to bruise
Maybe a slight injury, you probably could deny
Or perhaps a painful sorrow a child would die
The gun is for protection, not to be used recklessly
Or does it make you feel powerful while others feel helpless
If no training you have don't pick up the gun
The next life you take could be your love one.

A Joyous Day

Feel the joy, feel the gladness
Enjoy the moment, forget the madness
The heart sounds a rhythmic beat
Life is stressful, you feel the heat
So rise early in the morning
To another day the sun's adorning
Be kind to those you pass along the way
Bid them God's speed and for them pray
Be thankful for the blessing you have received
For someone will see your gratefulness and they too will believe

A Love No More

A love once filled my heart is no more
Joyful memories lie deep upon the ocean's floor
Moonlight walks, hand in hand
Bare feet gliding through the island's sand
Your eyes closed, yet I, you could see
Your lips soft, warm kisses, passionately
You held me tight, you held me close
My love you received, your love you gave
As life is, time revealed its boldest face
The distance between us formed a solid place
I tried to hold on, but you let go
A forgotten heart, a love no more

A Prayer

When I open my eyes at the dawning of a new day
I whisper a prayer to God and say
Father, I thank you for all the blessings you've given to me
Thank you for all the things I see
You've allowed me to taste the good of the land
You help me to feel and touch others with my hand
I appreciate the ability to hear the birds singing the morning song.
Thank you for the smell of life for some day it will be gone.
Thank you for forgiveness, for my sins he hung on the cross
Eternal life I'll gain, I could not repay the cost.
But thank you for the gift of your name I can call
To you be glory, dominion, and power forever, Amen

A Simple Question

What is life without God?
How can we live without a supreme being?
Have anyone seen him face to face?
Is there true evidence that He is great as they say He is?
Is the faith that you have in him real or learned?
Is the baggage of life part of a plan to be reconciled back to Him?
Does he live on earth, in heaven, or in us?
Is he known by any other name?
How many are one God?

A True Man of God

A Shepherd,
Leading God's people to the kingdom,
He was Anointed!

A Leader,
Equipping the saints for the work of the ministry,
He was Appointed!

A Comforter,
Showing compassion, brotherly love and unmerited acts of
kindness,
He was Called!

A Friend,
Extending a gentle hand, a strong shoulder, an encouraging
word,
He was Chosen!

A gift from heaven stands firm in our midst,
An angel of Christ, one who was sent to assist.
One who boldly declares the word of the Lord,
Which cuts us deeply like a two edged sword.
He gives of his time, he gives from his heart,
No change found in him, he's the same from the start.
With his life, God's purpose he is fulfilling,
For he has yielded his vessel, and his heart is willing,
To be, a true man of God.

Be Free

Freedom comes in your live as you let the past go
Which means anything that happen just a minute before
The final release of things that had you bound
With the fragmented thoughts in your head spinning around
Get focused on the future because love is yet ahead
No more sadness or tears, no more of the dread
Appreciate each day you are blessed to open your eyes
Each day is a challenge take it as no surprise

Blessed Like That

Blessings from the Lord always amazes me
I stand in awe how they come unexpectedly
Never could I imagine the magnitude of his gifts
I was ecstatic, my heart, my spirit, my soul did he lift
I heard his voice say "wait" when I felt no one cared
I heard him say "be still", for I am always there
Those things I had lost now seem so minute and small
For God began to restore when upon his name I called
I saw him build me a house, no money did I have to buy
I felt him dry my tears for all I did was cry
He freed my sisters out of church bondage imposed by man
I saw him save the other one by his almighty hand
I saw him bless my two sons with reassurance and peace
I felt him remove the pain oh what a wonderful release
By his grace, he gave me a compassionate heart
To help those who lives had be ripped and torn apart
Even though in life, things are taken from us as we try to live
But always remember, God blesses, restores and forgive.

Call Me Healed

I've been knocked down, I've been pushed around,
I've had my face slapped, my smile turned upside down.

I've been called names which didn't sound the same as my mother
called me.

I've been lied too, I've been evilly spoken too,
I've had to laugh when inside I felt only blue.

I've been called names which didn't sound the same as my mother
called me.

I've found the strength, I've found the faith to get up and remove
myself from that place.

Today, by His grace, I have a healed heart.
Got a new lease on life, got a fresh start.

Now, I am called by the name that sounds the same as my mother
called me.

Call of Love

Sitting here, my heart ponders and wait
It waits for a true call of love

I'm still, I'm quiet, and I'm calm
Patience is a virtue, how long is the wait for love

I yearn for your hand to draw me close
To transcend the force of a mere friendship

To ride the waves of life for a time emerged
My desire, to see the glow upon your face

When you answer the call to be king of my life
You'll stand strong, passion will defeat desire,

Love reigns, my heart forever content.

Child's Desire

He's coming for sure, my mommy said,
I waited patiently by the door, no knock, no word.
The emptiness of his presence was felt with pain,
Cause my daddy, I hate to say, lied again.
I know he'll come soon, I tell my mind.
But his interest is, shooting the breeze with friends, killing time.
He's caught in the place of delayed responsibility,
exemplifying his weakness, not abilities.
I find it somewhat hard to grasp as a child,
Why my daddy won't settle down, why he's so wild.
If I but a chance to touch his life,
I'll show him happiness and joy, not strife.
I'll give him all my love I have inside,
helping him to know, he's all to me,
and he could be to me, all the dad I need him to be.

Childhood Friends

Have you ever thought about your childhood friend?
Whether life's been good to them or if they're at life's end.
The days of old, when you played in the burning sun.
Now the night seem cold and no one is having fun.
How you rode our bikes, how you splashed in the mud.
How you use to fight and then you would hug.
You pinky swore to be friends until death do you part.
For I'll forever hold, my childhood friend memories,
in my heart.

Church People

In the church,
>   There are saints that come to worship and praise
>   Others come to stare and gaze
Which one are you?

In the church,
>   There are some spirit-filled deacons
>   Others are demon-possessed sneaks
Which one are you?

In the church,
>   There are some true members
>   Others come to disassemble
Which one are you?

In the church,
>   There are the holy mothers
>   Others are noisy mothers
Which one are you?

In the church,
>   There are those who do the mission work
>   Others who work the mission
Which one are you?

In the church,
>   There are singers who can croan
>   Others who can barely moan
Which one are you?

In the church,
>There are those pastors true to the calling
>Others just keep right on falling

Which one are you?

Our place of worship is where the spirit of the Lord is presence
It's where we find our peace and strength
Lets keep it a Holy Place.

Come Now Chillun

Come now chillun, like I said
Ma done made dat lasses and bread
All you gone eat, fo you go to sleep
Cause I'm gone peek when you try to sneak
Dat lasses and bread
I done thro a shoe upside dat head.

In memory of my granddaddy!

Couples Together

Look at the couples who are together as they share a warm embrace
How fascinating it is to watch how love will illuminate ones face
They express without words the sentiments of their hearts
A love rooted so deeply never to depart

Emotions Design

Emotions of happiness unfolds all in a season,
Without warning love was, for no apparent reason.
The highlight of passion, raged like a troubled river,
while ecstasy filled the air, causing the body to quiver.
Acts of giving, never being refused or limited,
the imagination create its own design, uninhibited.
Then love explodes freely, the expression, a jovial sigh.
But the seed of devotion and commitment dissolves
And the designer is questioning the why.

Free Love

A dream of love is overcast by the shadow
of the still blue sea.

The dark shine dances quietly through the night.

The thoughts are yet peaceful and undisturbed.
Is there a free love, no frustrations,
problems, or confusion?
Can love be preserved through these things?

Yes, as long as, the overcast of the still blue sea,
is greater than, the shadow of the dark night.

For Gertha, My Sister

You have a way about you that makes everyone glow,
A pleasing personality, all your sisters know.

You're always there and willing to do for me,
Whatever I need or whatever I request of thee.

You must realize, I'm not the only sister who feels this way,
But all five of us, just ask, and we will say.

You are our world's most precious treasure!
We have a love for you that is beyond measure!

For Real

How do you know when someone's for real
Do you gage life by what you know or what you feel
People often show the face they want you to see
Hiding their true selves from you and me
When you finally realize what you've seen is so unreal
Broken emotions, hurt feelings, with all this you must deal
So never override those feeling of warning you feel inside
You will soon find out the person has much to hide.

Grandma's Words

Who can ever forget Grandma's words, a gift forever embedded in
    our minds.
Words never to be erased, not even by time.
Words of wisdom, to guide us through each day we face.
Words of encouragement, allowing us to go through with grace.
Words of correction, while on the path we stray.
Words of love, teaching us to kneel and pray.
Words to uplift our spirits, when our countenance is downward,
Words to unite us when in our family there is mere discord.
Words of hope, if ever we find ourselves in despair,
Words of peace, when confused, the Savior our burden he'll bare.
Grandma's words are a hidden treasure, to sustain and uphold,
She received the same gift from her grandmother, I'm told

Green Bird

Green bird, Green bird, why are you sitting there?
You have no worries. You have no cares.
Your feathers glows as the sun upon them shine
You looked pretty friendly as you sit on the pine
Green bird, green bird do you sing as the sun rise
Or do you just sit there blinking your tiny eyes
I may not know all the things you do
The green you wear is beautiful, that much is true.

Hard Headed Child

Why worry about a hard-headed child?
Mean, stubborn, irresponsible and wild
Don't listen, talk back, lazy and slack
No school, no rules, thinking all is cool
Hanging in the streets with others like them
Cursing, fighting, pants dropped, buying rims
No training, no skills, on you they will live
Baby mama drama with nothing to give
A hard-headed child will live only half of their days
If they don't listen and change their ways

Kenneth Go to Bed

I sent him to bed at nine each night
Yet he's standing in his door and on pops the light
His plan is to come and sleep in my room
But I'm standing in the door full of gloom
Saying Kenneth please go to bed
I took him by his ear pulling it a bit hard
He tripped on the floor hitting his forehead
He broke a tooth and busted his lip
I didn't mean for him to get hurt he just slipped
Now he's crying and can't sleep
For he is in pain but I have to weep
Sure he has his own thought and mind
But he won't know he's lost rest until morning time

Leah a Gift

It was five days before the celebration of Jesus' birth,
When God commanded his archangel to summon earth.

The request was to find the most precious jewel in the land,
To be presented as his son's gift, his demand.

So the archangel obeyed as he was told, for obedience
was a must, not that he was so bold.

During the search, he saw many jewels that night, but
not one as tiny, beautiful, precious to his sight.

The beauty the angel beheld was like no other, known only
to her father, mother, and brother.

Now his majestic will is justified, the most precious jewel,
Leah, is by his side.

A new life for her, now unfolds, forever unknown to man.
She now walks with Christ, hand in hand.

Life is a Song

Life is but a love song expressed within the heart.
Life is but a sad song when our love ones depart.
Life is but a song of hope when your light seems dim.
Life is but a song of peace only when you look to him.

Love Is

Like a flower, blooming in its season, love is.
Like the rain, pouring gently upon the ground, love is.
Like the grass glowing greener than its color, love is.
Like the ocean, tossing its waves higher than ever, love is.
Like a storm, raging under the dark booming clouds, love is.
Love is all that you think it is, love is everything.

Love Tease

Have you ever loved someone and they did not love you?
Wanting them so badly, you knew not what to do.
You thought about the things, you thought would get their attention.
Nothing worked, their interest, no longer exist, not to mention.
I tried to give them my best so they would be pleased.
Effortless, just useless, myself only did I tease.
I refrained, hoping it would draw them closer.
Their head turned further, I felt a bad choice.
Finally I told myself, to him, I could just be a friend.
My mind told me, I love him to the end.
To love is to give, to have is to hold,
To live is to release them from your soul.

My True Friend!

My true friend was there when things fell apart,
My true friend opened up their heart.
My true friend lended a helping hand,
My true friend was there when I could not stand.
My true friend ignored the lies that was told,
My true friend was with me, oh how bold.
My true friend treats me the same whether near or far,
My true friend encourages me, I'm their star.
My true friend loves me without a doubt I know.
If you are my true friend, why doesn't it show?

Nature's Right

A mass of great water, the beautiful ocean is
Undeniable breathless from the array it gives
One stand for hours gazing as far as the eyes can see
Who thinks of disaster or even a great Tsunami
Rippling from Asia to Africa, the true motherland
With gigantic force ever too strong for man
Unexpectedly the waves danced like giants in the air
Upon the earth, it drew lives back to the ocean floor, nothing to spare
Families separated and many lives lost
Many countries sent aide, what an enormous cost
It is nature's right to do as nature will
The result devastation, then return the ocean to a calming still.

Ole Road of Life

Ole road of life, which path must I take?
To refrain from wandering needlessly,
the choice is it mine to make?
The way to follow should be clear,
no doubt in mind or heart.
Any cloudiness in thinking,
would lead to endless distraught.

I wish to travel a plain path,
stretching broad and long.
With love, hope and charity
abundantly adorned.
I hope to lend a hand, if ever the time a rise,
to someone in need of help,
less my offer they despise.

Never could I choose the right path,
without seeking help from my guide.
The One I put my trust in,
The One in whom I abide.
So at the fork, on the ole road of life,
I'm sure myself will be,
But never deciding alone,
I'll be consulting his MAJESTY.

Our God

We worship you, we adore you our God
We give you the glory, the honor, our God
Our hands are lifted, in praise, you're our treasure
None like you, can't compare, nor measure

We give you praise our God
We give you praise our God

We worship you, we adore you, our God

Jehovah you are God, Jehovah you are God
Your righteousness is perfect in all its ways
We give you glory, honor and praise.

We worship, we adore you, our God
We worship, we adore you, our God.

Party Pain

We made a choice to go out to the party,
Ready to dropped it like it's hot, hearty hearty.
We talked about our next move,
How the music would be blasting, how we would grove.
Got there, crowd too big, had to bounce.
My friend, with his gold chain, who knew the ounce.
On our way, strangers stopped us in our tracks,
Next thing I knew, hospitalized, wounded leg and back
But the most amazing thing for me,
None of this coming, I could see.
Heard there was a lot of shooting around the way
Didn't think it could happen to me, I would say
Now I know, miracles are for real,
Because I can still walk, I can still feel.
God spared my life during this Christmas season,
Now I owe him thanks and praise for this reason.
Lord, help me to realize, it was you who gave me another chance
To see my child grow, play and dance.
It just didn't happen and it just wasn't circumstance.

Peace of Son

In the midst of gray days lies sorrow, yet knowing behind the grayness
there awaits a brighter tomorrow. Never let your dreams vanish in a
cloudy thought. Who'll ever know what the next moment will bring.
For at the time of thinking to release life's rope, the treasurer
of peace comes, then there's hope. To face the challenges ahead,
one thing we must-learn how to love, learn how to trust.
Trust God in all things, he is first. Trust him for life's blessings
and you'll never thirst. If you stand firm on the truth of his word,
a day without sun will not seem so absurd. He is our help
when the sun doesn't shine. He is our strength,
our courage, our peace of mind.

Pride in Color

When I step into the world,
I step with my head held high.
When I face the world,
I reminisce of the colored women of years gone by. Those women,
who, carried the weight
of injustice upon their brow.
Those women, who, overcame the struggle,
unable to explain the how.

I find pride in knowing, I was one in whom they were
fighting for, determined not to settle for the less,
they knew we deserved much more.

We, the colored women, are too in God's blessing plan,
we were only deprived by the greed of man's hand.
But never use that truth to cause more despair, as we become
more blessed, our purpose is to share.

Sharing immensely, the baton of wisdom, strength and
courage, passing it from one colored woman,
to a woman of color.

Romance Buds

A romance budding like the pedals of a flower
Into the unknown it blooms in a timely hour
Chosen by fate we look for the other to know
What will be expected, how this romance will grow
We can only wait, for time alone has the answer
To the question, that lie within our minds,
If our heart will be as one, or if another you'll find
So let's enjoy the enjoyable, with laughter and glee
If nothing more, you've found a friend in me

So Long Friend

Trust me, the lips of the mouth chattered,
I confided in a friend and my world was shattered.
Like a broken mirror, I laid helplessly on my face,
my life upside down totally out of place.
The puzzle of my mind was scattered here and there,
a heart torn apart, does anybody care?
I heard friends were for keeps, what a hilarious thought,
now I know better, some friends are destined to depart.

Sounds of Fall

Ever walked toward the sun in the fall of the year
Ever notice the ever-changing sounds one might hear
In the air, the wind blowing swiftly through the trees
Upon the ground, the rustling of fallen leaves
Up above, a chirping bird, hidden by nature's color
In the distance, busy cars moving to and fro
Ever let your mind wonder while walking in the fall of the year
Sounds disappear, relaxation for the soul.

Street People

Who are the people walking along the streets, to and fro?
Why are they just walking, don't they have somewhere to go?
Mind you, everyday, the streets are on their schedule,
Most of them are out there because of life's failure.
In passing, a wave is the right thing to give,
Or they'll talk about the high life you live.
At sunrise, on the south end they'll hang for a while.
At sunset, the north end it will be, in a single file.
Don't approach them wrong, respect first, no doubt.
If not, insulted you'll get, simply cursed out.
Some are laid back, pants dropped, chilling, what a sight.
For some are homeless, the streets, is where they'll sleep tonight.
Is this lifestyle part of the Master's plan?
To beg, to borrow, always extending the hand.
Has hope escaped the essence of their mind, never to return?
Or have they used everyone, now all bridges are burned?
How can we help these people conform to the standard society has set?
Or should we leave them to the streets, alone, to pay their own debt?

The Burning Bush

You made the decision to send our troops to war,
Many are confused they don't understand what they are fighting for.
Going against men whose been fighting since the biblical days,
Our bombs don't scare them, they're on a mission, they don't sway.
From birth, the mission is embedded into their minds,
American can't defeat them, we're wasting money and time.
What is your true reason you sent our troops out to the sand,
More oil wells for you, more money in your hand.
9-11 enemies were Saudi's, little to do with Saddam and Iraq,
You tried to blind side the Americans and that's a known fact.
Those inspectors reported no weapons of mass destruction,
But you're convinced, its oil, to the desert were your instructions.
Your greed has caused more pain than you'll ever know,
Let's unrope the deal cowboy this is not a rodeo!
Oil means money and money just can't burn,
Many of our troops to homeland their never return.
Look at your own love ones, protected and all in one place,
While others are heart-broken, tears running down each face.
The House gave you a bill to slowly bring our troops home,
But you vetoed it and said Americans don't run!
RETURN OUR TROOPS HOME, this is Americans plead,
It falls on death ears, for the real cause of your war is greed!

The Clown

Someone sent me a clown, when I had nothing to laugh at, at all.
When my life was broken, my back against a wall.
Intensely the storm poured, the ice yet to melt.
Reminding me constantly of the discomfort I felt.
I could not comprehend the meaning of the clown's smile,
As, I blankly stared at him, much longer, than a while.
Then I realized the smile was a symbol, simply to be passed
around. A mere expression of God's grace, of how
He can turn any challenging situation upside down.

The Day America Turned to God
911

There's a song, which has a verse, saying "someone please call 911". As the day of 9-11 began, the evidence of man's unchanged heart was revealed, one still full of greed, hate and sin.

A day of explosion, chaos, trembling and fear.
A day of mourning, numbness, disbelief and tears.
A day that Death hung a banner across the nation.
In New York, D.C., Pennsylvania, sirens ringing from station to station.

God's name was called more times on 9-11 than any day before. He sat up upon the throne, saying, "Is that America knocking at my door." He began to rush to the door, but one angel said, "you may not want to answer too soon-YOU KNOW THEM-America will call you early in the morning and forget about you by noon". God replied to the angel "you may just be right, I think I'll let them bear the burden, just through the night." The sun rose again, God still heard America's voice, united in prayer, united, because we didn't have a choice. The reality of the 9-11 day had set in, man's heart, still full of sin.

Then God listened to the moaning and prayers, making sure it was He America needed, then he told his angel, "Yes, it is me on whom they are calling. I told them in my word, I am their GOD and they are my people. I told them, I would never leave them, nor forsake them. I also told them if they turned their hearts, seek my face and pray, I will heal their land." God's word is true, God is faithful to his promise. He will not leave us comfortless, He is the Comforter.

The Drunk Woman

Making her way across the street, staggering from one side to the
   other
A drunk woman, she's lost all virtue, she's a daughter perhaps
   someone's mother
You can see her along the way in every town, city and state
How did she get out there, world pleasure, or was it just fate
She walks along a destructive path on a road of no return
She's been out there for awhile, by now you'd think she'd learn
Whatever the reason is, the truth is she is there
Thinking not one soul love her, thinking no one cares
How can we help her to understand, drinking leads to a tragic end
There's no one she trust, not one on who she can depend
Life has dealt her a card, be it deal or not, that passed us by
But it's our helping hand to extend, its our duty to love, one we
   can't deny

The Hungry of America

America, our country, our land, and our home
Greater than any other, no matter where you roam
With phenomenon wealth, no country can compare
We got so much money, we've got money to spare
We've fed the hungry on every coast and land
So why are our children going hungry, with an empty hand
To encounter the feeling of hunger is horrible
To lie down to sleep without food is deplorable
We're quick to rush to any country's aide
Including those countries with huge debts unpaid
Our children they are hungry, some go without meals
Or has America turned her face, this problem is real
To maintain our great nation, we must invest in our young
Or America will be headed for the great plunge
If our own children are feed and nourished right
America will be fortified and gain strength overnight
America, this situation can't get any worst
Feeding our own children, should always be first.

The Passing

When our love ones pass away, we say life is so unfair,
We feel God doesn't love us, we feel he just don't care.
But we know those thoughts are not reality, it's not his nature at all,
For his promise is to comfort us and never let us fall.
We try to hold on to the memories of our friendship ever more,
We often wonder what's it like over there on the other shore.
It's not always an easy task to hold the pain and tears inside,
For they'll run down your face, you have to lose all pride.
We can never understand God's will, no sense it will ever seem,
But it surely feels better, when we know they're in the arms of the
      Redeemed!

The Power Within

From Adam's rib, God, did he create
A woman, a perfect design, not a single mistake
He empowered her with his Holy Spirit for life's completion
For he knew along the way many ills set to defeat us
Who else has the strength to travail through hardness of labor
Bringing little miracles in the world, we are chosen, God's favor
He gives us patience and compassion to be caring mothers
To uplift the lost soul, some are our sisters and brothers
He enables us wisdom and intellect, none by to measure
A gift, the indwelling of the spirit, our hidden treasure
He charges our live constantly to the throne of grace
This life we cannot live, unless we seek his face
The power within us is far greater than any ruby or pearl
It's the anointing of the spirit upon our lives, women, that
Is going to change this world

The Window of Yesteryear

Looking through the window of yesteryear
Find you there, men of hope, courage, no fear.

Saints ready to answer the call, all on one accord,
Willing to build a house for our Lord.

A place of refuge, a place of shelter, a place to worship in
So that lost souls, the sin sick, could come and be strengthened

I can see the righteous sending prayer heaven's way
For money was scarce, resources few, limited pay

With the spirit of Nehemiah embedded deeply within their heart
A mind to work, a mind to move forward, a mind to start

Through the window, I can see the naysayers whispering the work
Would never be complete
But they stayed on the wall, they worked for hours, some did not eat

Through the window, I see many who preached, taught and even
        screamed
Leading God's people to repentance, that they might be redeemed

From then to now, God's spirit has held St. Augusta together
Although firey destruction, division, the stormy times, St. Augusta
        did weather

For the remnant of St. Augusta is still building on a strong
        foundation
The solid rock Jesus, he is our one and only true salvation

The Wrong Crowd

Tonight will be a night, like all other nights,
my mom she'll get dressed and be out of sight.

She's going out to party of course, with the wrong crowd,
dancing, gambling, and smoking, being oh so loud.

She doesn't have my needs or desires on her mind at all,
for to be all that to friends, are most important, got to have a ball.

She doesn't realize I depend on her so much,
to be a mother to me, I need a mother's loving touch.

I want to feel the warmth of a caring mother,
not some old scary looking stranger or perhaps her significant other.

I go to school each day with my smile upside down,
cause my mother, has been nowhere around.

I bet if I ask the crowd on the corner, if they've seen or heard,
they would say, sure have, and that's word!

Mother when will you realize, I'm just a growing child,
and I'll learn nothing from you except how to be wild.

Do you even think one day, I might be hanging out there,
full of despair, lost, with no one to care.

I want to grow up to be, all God intended for me,
not someone without hope, peace or charity.

Our best time together is passing both of us by,
for when our time is over there will be no need to cry.

Today, I wish you would think, what's best for me,
for the crowd that you hang with, is not the best, you'll see.

Walking in the Light

Walk in the light where you will find joy everlasting
In the light there is peace for the asking
Love is there, uncompromised, given through the promise
The light brightens even the darkest of places
Where there is gloom, the light overshadows, then erases it
If there is doubt the light pierces and destroys it
If there is worry the light will replace it
He is the light of the world
For the word tell of his truth
Look to the light and life will have more meaning to you.

With You

Take me to a foreign place, to find my love, one who will be there.
Fly me high above the cloud, to find my love, one who will care.

MY LOVE, he will lead my hand, as we meringue, salsa in the sand.
The giant wave roll of the tide, as he holds me close to his side.
Constantly kissing me on my lips and upon my face.
Hoping in his heart, I'll find a secure place.

So when I return to the home of the brave and land of the free,
My heart will remain, where it will always be, WITH YOU.

To Antonio, con besos, Donna!

Yet I Survived

When I needed you most, you left me, yet I survived.
Oh the numbness, I felt, was I even alive?
My countenance revealing only a blank stare,
Drifting, wandering, going nowhere.
I reached for the Word, for my spirit to be filled.
But my heart was overwhelmed, my spirit, I could not yield.
I laid upon my face, praying to the Lord,
I simply give up, this life, it's too hard.
But I continued to cry out, my soul he did restore
Now I trust in him faithfully, my everlasting Lord.
He comforted me, the times I was going through.
That is one of the promises, he said he would do.

You

You drew me near, you lead the way
You touched my face, you kissed my feet
You talked to me, you listened to me
You encouraged me, you secured me
You let me see the sunrise, you let me see the sunset
You prayed with me, you praised with me
You laughed with me, you cried with me
You cared for me, you loved me
Then
You left me!

Zariah

Mom lies there travailing, her time draws near,
Patiently waiting for my first grandchild, oh my dear.
We encourage to focus, not much longer we say.
The doctor say push, we gather around and wait,
For Zariah Presleigh to come, she's already late.
Slowly she peeps from the darkness of her mother's womb,
Mother's now tired ready for all to leave the room.
Her head, full of hair, eyes wide and bright,
Crying willfully, oh what a beautiful sight.
They gave her to her mother she placed her upon her breast,
Then passes her to her father, he places her up on his chest.
With love and adoration, we praise God for just for a little while,
Thanking him for this miracle, my first grandchild!